5 THINGS ANYONE CAN DO TO
HELP START A CHURCH

5 THINGS ANYONE CAN DO TO
HELP START A CHURCH

PHIL STEVENSON

wesleyan
publishing
house

Indianapolis, Indiana

Copyright © 2008 by Wesleyan Publishing House
Published by Wesleyan Publishing House
Indianapolis, Indiana 46250
Printed in the United States of America
ISBN: 978-0-89827-382-3

All Scripture quotations, unless otherwise indicated, are taken from the HOLY BIBLE, NEW INTERNATIONAL VERSION ®. NIV ®. Copyright 1973, 1978, 1984 by the International Bible Society. Used by permission of Zondervan Publishing House. All rights reserved.

Scripture quotations marked (KJV) are taken from THE HOLY BIBLE, King JAMES VERSION.

All rights reserved. No part of this publication may be reproduced, stored in a retrieval system, or transmitted in any form or by any means—electronic, mechanical, photocopy, recording or any other—except for brief quotations in printed reviews, without the prior written permission of the publisher.

CONTENTS

You Can Help Start a Church!   6

1 GO PUBLIC   10

2 GENERATE PRAYER   25

3 GIVE PROMOTION   42

4 GENEROUSLY PROVIDE   59

5 GRANT PERMISSION   77

Notes   95

YOU CAN HELP START A CHURCH!

We did not want to have an evangelistic strategy for our church that did not include the most effective evangelistic strategy, which is church multiplication.
Blair Ritchey

It is God's design that all things multiply according to their own kind, as we see in the biblical account of creation. Seeds produce the kinds of plants and trees from which they came. Their seeds in turn produce plants and trees of like kind. God made all sorts of wild animals, and they have reproduced more of their own kinds (see Gen. 1:11, 12, 25). It is not difficult to apply this concept to the church. If God's design was to multiply in like kind, why wouldn't the church also multiply itself? Because the church is a living body, it should be reproducing itself.

Believers should multiply believers, and churches should multiply churches. This is what the church at Antioch understood—and did—when it commissioned Paul and Barnabas (Acts 13:1–3). "The earliest churches obeyed the

Great Commission by planting new congregations to carry out the assignments of discipline, baptizing, and teaching that would begin the multiplication process of planting more and more churches."[1] This is missional multiplication.

We will never have a genuine missional multiplication movement if it is not spearheaded by the local church. Denominations do not effectively plant churches. Area judicatories do not effectively plant churches. It is the responsibility of existing churches to multiply. Local churches have lost their missional mindset.

At a conference I attended, Tom Clegg made the following observation: "Believers have gotten out of the believer multiplication business, so churches have stepped in to multiply believers. This has resulted in churches getting out of the church multiplication business, so judicatories have attempted to multiply churches. Believers need to multiply believers and churches need to multiply churches." Clegg is correct. The church needs to get back to leading the charge in starting churches. Local leaders must no longer abdicate their responsibility of church multiplication to area judicatory or denomination leaders. And judicatory leaders must resist the temptation to pick up the mantle dropped by the local church.

George Bullard says two things must be in place for a church planting movement to occur: (1) a denomination must be planting 5 percent, or more, of the number of existing churches, and (2) this must be a grassroots movement bubbling up from local churches. Churches plant churches, and denominations create an environment for this to happen.

We need churches to plant churches! A denomination can create the spiritual and strategic environment for this, but churches need to plant churches. For many local church leaders the initial response to the idea of starting a new church is, "No way!" They don't believe they have whatever it takes to help start a new church. They aren't sure what that whatever is, but they're sure they don't have it.

The truth is, every church, regardless of size or location, can help start new churches. A church that believes in church planting will find a way to participate in church planting.

When I was a freshman in high school, I was working out in the weight room on a Universal Gym. Although I had limited experience in weight training, I knew a little about this one unit that was comprised of several stations. Each station worked a specified set of muscles. You could adjust the weights by relocating a pin to designated spots on a stack of weights. I was working the bench press, and had the pin located in the double digits. A fellow athlete entered the room. He observed what I was doing. I completed my exercise. Without asking he pulled the pin and moved it to a higher weight (triple digits).

"There!" he said. "Try that." He was a year older, so I felt it not wise to argue—although I was sure I would not be able to lift the new weight. To my surprise I lifted it easily. Then he said, "See! You can do more than you think you can."

The same is true for you and your church. You can do more than you think you can. You can help start new churches. You can make a difference.

In the following pages you will find five suggestions on how to participate in church planting. I call these the "GPs": Go Public, Generate Prayer, Give Promotion, Generously Provide, and Grant Permission. Do these five things and let the multiplication movement begin!

1
GO PUBLIC

I served on staff at Skyline Church in San Diego for six years. Under the tutelage of John Maxwell, I learned many key leadership principles. One was: "What gets rewarded is what gets done."

One form of reward is affirmation. We clap and cheer for the small steps a baby takes. We cheer when our team scores. Preachers appreciate an "amen" at key moments of a sermon. Everyone enjoys the kind words of another regarding something he or she has done or become. I know how much I appreciated compliments received when I had a recent weight loss.

I've heard it said that John Wooden, the legendary UCLA basketball coach, instructed his players to always acknowledge the person who passed them the ball that resulted in a score. It could be a smile, a wink, or a nod—anything to affirm their participation. One of his players asked, "But coach, what if he's not looking?" Wooden responded, "I guarantee he'll look. If he's not looking, I will be." He understood the significance of affirmation.

Affirmation does two things. First, it confirms and firms up a choice. It reminds us of why we are doing what we are doing. Second, it keeps us moving. Affirmation is motivational. It enables us to continue when a course becomes difficult.

I have a friend who is a marathoner. He has participated in at least a dozen of these runs. In 2006 my wife and I went to Chicago to watch him run in the Chicago Marathon. There were thousands of runners. There also were thousands of affirmers. Affirmers were those who lined the course as we did, calling out encouragement to any and all who passed. This affirmation confirmed each runner's decision to participate and kept them all running as the race became more difficult.

Affirmation is critical, but there is an affirmation enhancer. This enhancer is the willingness to go public. That is—being vocal about the affirmation. It would have been one thing for my wife and me to appreciate the runners in our thoughts, but it made a difference when we became vocal. An unspoken affirmation is no affirmation at all.

Going public about supporting church planting is the first thing anyone can do to help start a new church. Public affirmation of starting new churches begins to engage the imagination of a congregation. Awareness of the need to begin new churches raises interest in the local church. When we are aware, we may not act; but if we are never aware, action isn't even an option.

> "We can't all be heroes because someone has to sit on the curb and clap as they go by."
> Will Rogers

LEADING OFF

In baseball, lead-off hitters are critical. They are first in the batter's box. They set the pace. Teams are looking for lead-off hitters who can make contact with the ball, get on base, and quickly get in a position to help the team get runs. Why? Runs win games.

The pastor and leadership team are the lead-off hitters. They must affirm their support of church planting. If the leaders don't go public with their desire to help begin churches, the people will not respond. Going public (getting on base) begins with the pastor. He or she must own the willingness to help start new churches.

Often pastors are Zechariah leaders. Zechariah was a priest (and the father of John the Baptist) who was unable to speak until the birth of his son. He had this wonderful insight from God, but was unable to share it with anyone. This is what Zechariah leaders do. They have a dream, but they keep it to themselves. Unlike the priest, it is not that Zechariah leaders can't speak; it's that they choose not to speak.

> Everyone ought to plant a tree under whose shade he will never sit.

People will never connect with what they don't hear. The leader must go public with the dream to start churches. But first the leader must catch the dream. Only then can it be shared. And a dream shared is a dream owned.

CATCH THE DREAM

A dream is the result of seeing needs. There is a critical need for new churches. According to Dave Olson of theamericanchurch.org, church attendance is not keeping up with population growth. We will need twenty-three hundred churches started each year to keep up with population growth.[1]

> Established churches are declining in attendance by 1–2 percent per year.

Olson observes that, "Established churches are declining in attendance by 1–2 percent per year."[2] New churches attract new people and have better effectiveness in reaching unchurched folks.

Ed Stetzer, in his book *Planting New Churches in a Postmodern Age*, states that churches under three years of age win an average of ten people to Christ per year for every one hundred members. Churches that are three to fifteen years old win an average of five people per year for every one hundred members; and churches fifteen plus years of age win an average of three people per year for every one hundred members.[3]

As you can see from these statistics, church planting is a viable evangelistic strategy. Evangelistic churches ought to participate in this effective strategy because existing churches have what it takes to help start new churches: people, finances, leadership, resources, and structure.

> "Every church can, and should, be a strategic player in the fulfillment of the Great Commission through starting and multiplying new congregations."
>
> Robert Logan

New churches can be a wonderful extension of an existing church's ministry. If reaching people for Christ and connecting them to a community of believers is a critical aspect of your ministry DNA, starting new churches would be a marvelous method of living this out. Starting new churches is a critical vehicle for Great Commission ministry that challenges us to go into the world.

Is the dream beginning to stir in your heart? If so, you may find yourself wrestling with the following issues:

- A burden for the disconnected people of your region.
- You see new communities springing up and you are asking, "What can be done to reach them?"
- You have a deepening desire to get your church looking outside itself.
- You tire of your ministry effectiveness being tied to how many show up on Sunday morning.
- You have a limited acreage and it is too expensive to relocate.
- There is an ethnic community near you, and you are aware they will never integrate into your church.
- You have a number of people who are driving thirty minutes, one way, to church, and you know you will probably never get their neighbors in the door.

These are indicators that God may be stirring your heart to lead your church in starting a new church. Don't ignore them. Instead, explore them. Research some churches that are planting other churches. Spend time listening to God. Increase your passion for those disconnected from Christ. A willingness to start new churches is a result of a passion for lost people and time spent in prayer.

In a lecture at the American Society of Church Growth, George Hunter spoke on churches that effectively reach pre-Christian people. One characteristic is that they grow through proliferation. Hunter said a church that effectively reaches pre-Christians moves beyond addition and embraces multiplication. This is multiplication of small groups, large groups, members, disciples, and congregations. An effective church will recognize that it can never adequately reach all groups of people, but it can help start new congregations that can.

> Passion dictates priority.

A church will affirm its priorities. The leaders, especially the pastor, must allow the Spirit space to stir this passion in the hearts of the people of the congregation. This is best done through spending time with God, and seeing the needs in your ministry field.

> It takes all kinds of churches to start all kinds of churches to reach all kinds of people.

SPENDING TIME WITH GOD

We must not complicate this. Spending time with God is just that: spending time with God. It is making the time, taking the time, and spending the time. Time with God doesn't just happen. It has to be scheduled. Some believe scheduling time with God erodes its spiritual aspect. I disagree. What erodes the spiritual aspect of our relationship with God is not spending time with him.

The following are some guidelines to spending time with God.

Be Consistent. You'd probably agree that exercise is needed for physical fitness. You'd also probably agree that consistent exercise is preferable over sporadic physical activity. Similarly, regular, consistent quiet times with God would be more helpful than occasional attempts at connecting.

Discover Your Spiritual Sweet Spot. This is where you best connect with God. God has created each of us differently. Too often we have built our spiritual development on something we have read or heard someone say. They typically tell us what works for them. We attempt this only to see it wane. It could be equated with David attempting to fight Goliath with Saul's armor. It seemed to make sense, but it wouldn't produce results. Find how you best connect with God and do it consistently.

Use Variety. We don't get extra spiritual credit for drab spirituality. Get with God in a variety of locations. I like to go to a Catholic retreat center once a month. The new environment is invigorating. Pray in a variety of positions: kneeling, standing, sitting, bowing, flat on your face, or lying on your back. Use a variety of spiritual disciplines.

Be Open to God's Promptings. God has much to say to us. Often we miss what he has to say due to lack of attentiveness. Listening is a lost aspect of spending time with God. But in listening we best sense what God might have for us.

In our time with God we can catch his heart for a world that is disconnected from him, disconnected from the One who sent Jesus into the world. God sending Jesus was an expression of his missional nature. God sent Jesus; Jesus, through his Spirit, sends us. Church planting, then, is a tangible expression of God's missional nature.

KEY POINTS
- Be consistent.
- Discover your spiritual sweet spot.
- Use variety.
- Be open to God's promptings.

SEEING THE NEEDS IN YOUR MINISTRY FIELD

In order to communicate effectively, church leaders must become aware of the needs that surround them and act to address them. Church leaders easily get caught up in the programs of the church to the extent that they neglect the people the church is supposed to reach. People should drive the agenda. When we see people, we seek methods to reach them.

If a leader wants to increase his or her need awareness level there are some simple ways to do this. Start by taking a walk.

Walk around your neighborhood or community and observe what people are doing. If possible, get a guest speaker to fill the pulpit this week and do this during Sunday worship. During your walk, or some other time, find a local coffee shop or café. Order a cup of coffee. Simply sip, listen, and watch. And finally, ask questions to get to know the people around you. Listen to their stories. I was at a conference once where a young pastor had gone into his neighborhood and asked non-church attendees why they didn't go to church. The number one reason: they didn't believe church attendance was required to be a religious person. This provided him a new insight into those to whom he wanted to minister.

Increased need awareness results in the discovery that we cannot meet all the needs in our ministry field. This can discourage us, or it can motivate us to help start a new church that will meet some of the needs we discovered.

AFFIRMING THE NEED FOR CHURCH PLANTING

Spending time with God and seeing needs are critical in getting leaders to the point of participating in helping start a new church. From this vantage point leadership can genuinely affirm the need for church planting. The leaders will, initially, be the primary affirmers. The result of their enthusiasm will be public affirmation for planting. There are a variety of ways to bring the idea of church planting to the congregations.

Talk About it From the Pulpit. The pulpit is a powerful tool in affirming the value of church planting. People know that what is shared from that platform is important. When it is highlighted from the pulpit, especially by the lead pastor, it carries significant impact.

List New Churches Being Started. Let the congregation know churches are being planted. Listing them in the bulletin, newsletter, or weekly email elevates their value.

Invite a Planter to Share. Do you know any church planters? It doesn't even have to be someone in your denominational family. Invite them in to share their story. Or, if you know of a church planter who has a DVD, show this in a worship service. Another variation would be to have a lay person who is helping, or has helped, start a church come and share from his or her perspective.

Weave Planting Stories Into Sermons. Stories of church plants and church planters are illustrations of faith, trust, courage, and evangelism. You don't have to be preaching on church planting to use a story about church planting.

Teach on the Book of Acts. The book is one long example of the early church in its intentional efforts to invade its culture. Use this book to highlight the role church planting plays in advancing the kingdom.

Highlight Church Plants in the Bulletin. List the new church's name, location, name of pastor, spouse, and children. List the number of people saved and baptized. Include a highlight of the past month. Use the same principles as when highlighting missionaries.

List Where New Churches are Needed. A list of potential locations for new churches lets the congregation know church planting is a viable way to reach a region.

> **KEY POINTS**
> - Talk about it from the pulpit
> - List new churches being started.
> - Invite a planter to share.
> - Weave planting stories into sermons.
> - Teach on the book of Acts.
> - Highlight church plants in the bulletin.
> - List where new churches are needed.

Fran Tarkenton is in the Pro Football Hall of Fame. He played quarterback for the Minnesota Vikings and led them to three Super Bowl appearances in the 1970s. In one game, Tarkenton called a play that required him to block. He made the block, and the play resulted in a touchdown. The Vikings won.

The day following the game, Fran and the rest of the team were watching game film. When the play with his touchdown opening block was shown, he expected a big pat on the back. After all, seldom is an NFL quarterback called on to block, and less often does he make the block. The pat, verbal or otherwise, never came.

After the meeting Tarkenton approached stoic head coach Bud Grant. "You saw my block, didn't you, Coach? How come you didn't say anything about it?"

Grant replied, "Sure, I saw the block. It was great. But you're always working hard out there, Fran. I figured I didn't need to tell you."

"Well," Tarkenton replied, "if you ever want me to block again, you do!"

Never assume anything. Your people will not naturally think in terms of church planting. You need to affirm this as an important value. Get creative. When you own the church planting dream, you will find ways to affirm its significance. And others will soon catch the visions.

DISCUSSION QUESTIONS

1. Describe your understanding of church planting.

2. If you were to publicly affirm church planting, what would you do?

3. What would keep your church from helping start a new church?

4. What would give you a better understanding of church planting?

ACTION STEPS

1. Read or listen to something relating to churches planting churches.

2. Take a listening retreat; write down your impressions.

3. Select one of the options from "Seeing the Needs" and do it.

4. Do a YouTube search for videos related to church planting.

5. Invite a church planter to share his or her story.

RESOURCES

- *10 of 300* CD available from the Department of Evangelism and Church Growth of The Wesleyan Church, 317.774.3900.
- *The Ripple Church* by Phil Stevenson.
- *Churches Planting Churches* by Robert Logan.
- *Let Go of the Ring* by Ralph Moore.
- Parent Network online: www.wesleyan.org/ecg.

GENERATE PRAYER 2

A story in *Time* magazine reports on procedures used by pilots when flying fifty-passenger Fokkers into Baghdad Airport. "To avoid being shot down by Iraqi insurgents, the pilot must stay at 30,000 ft. until the plane is directly over the Baghdad airport, then bank into a spiraling dive, straightening up just yards from the runway." The reporter states, "Many of our fellow passengers will be calling to their maker when the plane begins its hellish descent."[1] Desperation does demand prayer.

Prayer is a critical aspect for any church that chooses to participate in starting new congregations. The willingness to pray for planters and planting is critical to the effectiveness of new outposts. Regardless of the location or the size of your church, you can pray. But not just any kind of prayer; this needs to be missional prayer.

MISSIONAL PRAYER

Praying missionally is projecting outward. Often, our prayers are primarily about us, our needs, our circumstances, and our church. It doesn't take long for a typical prayer time to move inward. We ask God to help us grow, heal our ailments, solve our problems, or give us strength. There is nothing wrong with such endeavors, but it is easy for churches and their leaders to neglect prayer for others.

> Prayer changes hearts, prepares communities, and opens eyes to the starting of new churches.

Missional prayer helps turn our prayers inside out.

Missional prayer asks God to work outside the walls of our church. It is reaching beyond property lines. It is asking God to till the soil of unresponsive people, closed communities, and hardened attitudes. It is fulfilling the specific request of Jesus to "ask the Lord of the harvest, therefore, to send out workers into his harvest field" (Matt. 9:38).

Jesus understood that opportunity was not limited by potential, but by the number of workers. The harvest is here. The potential in communities is great. We need workers. We need churches willing to send people to begin new churches. We need harvest-minded congregations to pray for God to raise up harvest-minded workers.

Dawson Trotman said, "I believe the need of the hour is an army of soldiers dedicated to serve Jesus Christ getting the gospel to every creature."[2]

Missional prayer is directed, outwardly focused, mobilizing prayer. It is not necessarily intercessory prayer. An intercessor can pray missionally, but those who pray missionally do not have to be gifted intercessors. There are only two criteria for a church that desires to pray missionally: an evangelistic passion and a willingness to pray.

> "The greatest barriers to church planting are in the mind."
> — Peter Wagner

This kind of prayer connects a church to God's mission. Out of this connection, a body of believers gains wisdom and insight on how to become involved in starting new churches. Out of this connection, a church fans the flame of its evangelistic passion.

What gets prayed about tends to get done. A congregation that chooses

> The church must have an evangelistic passion and a willingness to pray.

to pray about church planting will find a way to get involved.

EVANGELISTIC PASSION

How do we get an evangelistic passion? I believe it is a result of spending time both with God and with unbelievers. God's heart for those who are disconnected from him motivated him to reach down into humanity. He stepped down so we might step up to a life-changing relationship. When we spend time with the God who has such a heart we catch this same desire to bring others to him.

We also need to spend time with those disconnected from God. It is easy for a church to become a *Gilligan's Island* church—a cadre of shipwrecked folks. The fictional TV show castaways made a life for themselves on the island on which they were marooned. Even though the world beyond their island was changing, they were content with what they had made. Churches do the same thing. They create a culture within a culture—an island. They make their way. They learn to live and dwell. The world may be changing around them, but they have their island.

- Increase evangelistic passion.
- Spend time with God.
- Spend time with those disconnected from God.

We need to get off the island. We need to find opportunities to interact with those far from God. This could be paying attention to the world as you are out and about. It may be getting involved in your community through the PTA, the Chamber of Commerce, service groups, youth athletic leagues, or a neighborhood group. When we mingle in the culture God sent his Son to die for, our passion to reach the unreached is increased.

WILLINGNESS TO PRAY

E. M. Bounds observed that prayer is not preparation for the battle; it is the battle. Mentally, I wholeheartedly believe this. But if you were to observe my ministry practice it would not be so evident. I tend to lean toward the strategic side of things—doing stuff and trusting God will bless it; planning things, believing God will redirect if I'm heading the wrong way. I think God does direct as we move.

The book of Proverbs tells us, "Commit to the Lord whatever you do, and your plans will succeed" (16:3), and, "In his heart a man plans his course, but the Lord determines his steps." (16:9). From this perspective, prayer dependence on God is interwoven with our plans and processes. I think we all want to develop a genuine prayer dependency, but most of us find it hard to believe that spending time in prayer is more valuable than some other form of action.

This being the case, placing prayer as a critical ingredient for starting new churches strikes many as a bit counterproductive. We feel the need to get out there and mobilize our people to catch the planting spirit. We need to jump in with both feet. We need to make opportunities if they are not being presented. It is up to us to convince our people. We know that it is God's desire that all people be saved. And we are convinced that church planting is an effective way to bring the salvation message. Therefore, we need to get to it. If we do that, God will honor our initiative.

Yes, God desires all to be saved. But to jump in without preparing the soil of people's souls (both those inside and outside the church) will result in a difficult harvest. Prayer is the soul-soil preparation for planting.

A church that willingly prays for friends and family who don't know Christ; the church that prays for its community to be softened by the Spirit; the church that asks God to open its corporate eyes to areas that need a new outpost; the church that allows God to break its heart for broken people, is a church that will be an active participant in the starting of new churches.

Why does prayer do this? In the *Let Prayer Change Your Life Workbook*, Becky Tirabassi identifies six things prayer does:

1. Prayer fuels faith.
2. Prayer draws us to the Word to hear from God.
3. Prayer teaches us to trust God.
4. Prayer reveals God's plan and purpose for us.
5. Prayer releases God's power.
6. Prayer unleashes love for God.[3]

A missionally praying church will cultivate these six things in its corporate life. A church may help start new churches without prayer, but a church that does not pray will never really consider what God might have them do in starting new churches. A non-praying church that undertakes a plant will only do the human side of the endeavor. It will determine what can be done comfortably, what fits the budget, and what conforms to its existing concept of church. It is in prayer that a church is stretched to trust beyond budgets, tangible resources, and existing methods. Prayer is the planting enhancer.

THE SPEED OF THE LEADER

The speed of the team is the speed of the leader. This may not be true in every situation, but I believe it to be mostly true in prayer. The leader and leadership must cultivate their inner souls if they are to lead the church in praying for mission. This is difficult as most leaders are not naturally bent toward the gardening of their inner spiritual life. Leaders prefer checking off a list of goals achieved or tasks completed. Visible achievements offer leaders the most confirmation. Yet personal development requires quiet, reflective moments. Investing in time away to cultivate one's soul is a choice many leaders are unwilling to make.

If leaders are serious about leading a congregation in a genuine missional prayer emphasis, they must begin with themselves. Here are some suggestions that will help you farm the soil of your life.

Seek God Honestly. This is being honest about who you are. It is being honest about how you best experience God. It is being honest about seeking God for his own merit, rather than seeking a story of a God-encounter to pass along.

Spend Time in Your Garage. I am not a garage guy. I don't have a workbench. I don't have a huge set of tools. The garage is not my sanctuary. About the only thing I do in my garage is park my car, store my stuff, and get my lawnmower read to cut my lawn. I have friends who are garage guys. They paint the floor to protect the porous cement from spills. They spend time just being . . . there! Here's the thing: both their garages and mine are used for the owner's purposes. Similarly, we will all have different ways to arrange and use our time with God. I approach my time with God as an opportunity to connect in order to gain the resources needed to head out and engage in my calling. Others tend to enjoy time simply basking in God's presence. It is a time to retool personally before engaging in the task ahead. The fact is that we each need to determine how we will spend that time. How it gets arranged—like a garage—isn't the issue. The issue is whether or not it prepares us for what we are called to do.

See God in the Common Moments. God does not live in the church building. He is in, around, over, in front of, and behind us. When we begin to see God in the common places, at common times, it enhances our confidence level. Life is a collection of common moments that combine to create an extraordinary event; but for every day at Disney World there are hundreds of days of cleaning house. In life, we need to connect with God in the everyday and lead from that base.

Surrender, But Never Give Up. Often we ask God to provide the resources for our vision, but expect him to do so on our schedule. We need to be willing to surrender our work, our schedule, and our priorities. When we do this, God creates an environment of responsiveness in our lives and in the life of the congregation.

Step Out. It's important to step out, even though you might get stepped on. Leading a church toward starting a new church is not easy. But as you cultivate your listening heart through prayer, you will be more responsive to the Spirit's promptings. You will step out because you will know that you are where God wants you to be. People may misunderstand your actions, but you will step out anyway.

KEY POINTS
- Seek God honestly.
- Spend time in your garage.
- See God in the common moments.
- Surrender, but never give up.
- Step out.
- You won't get it all right.

You Won't Get it All Right. Try as you might, you'll never get it all right in life. If you think you will always make the right decisions, if you believe your plan will be flawless every time, if you have the mindset that your insights are beyond question then let me help you—forget about it! You will not get everything right. You will choose wrongly. Get over it, and get on with it! Living in the amazing grace of God allows us freedom to not always get it right. Living in the amazing grace of God provides us with the ability to remain humble when we do get it right.

Mobilize the people of your church to missional praying. Push them past the status quo of prayer. Engage them in the real work of prayer that both breaks their hearts for the lost and breaks the hard ground of resistance to the gospel. A church that prays missionally will soon become a church that seeks to involve itself in the starting of new congregations. There is a difference between believing that prayer is important and believing it is essential. Essential means there are things that will not happen without prayer. Prayer is essential for starting new churches.

IMPLEMENTING PRAYER

Living in Indiana, I have had to make several adjustments to the variety of weather conditions—most of which I never had to consider while growing up in Southern California. One of these weather anomalies is tornados. They can come quickly. Even with the warning systems, people can be caught off guard.

A mom and son were outside when a tornado surprised them. The mother clung to a tree and tried to hold her son. But the swirling winds carried him into the sky. He was gone.

The woman began to weep and pray: "Please, Lord, bring back my boy! He's all I have. I'd do anything not to lose him. If you'll bring him back, I'll serve you all my days."

Suddenly the boy toppled from the sky, right at her feet— a bit mussed up, but safe and sound. His mother joyfully brushed him off.

Then she stopped, looked to the sky, and said, "He had a hat, Lord."

Accuracy of this story notwithstanding, it does illustrate that when we begin to ask specifically, specific things happen. It may not end exactly as we anticipated, but it does have a positive outcome. We need to mobilize our congregations to ask specifically, regularly, and innovatively for church planting. What might God have for us to do? What resources do we have that might be helpful in planting churches? What locations are in need of new churches? What people are we not reaching that a different kind of church might reach?

The following are some suggestions as to how a church might involve itself in praying missionally for church multiplication:

- Make church planting a regular part of pastoral prayer. Many churches use pastoral prayer time for those sick or incapacitated. Why not add prayer for a church planter and the community when a new church is starting?
- Include the needs of church planters in your bulletin prayer section. List the names of those involved in church planting that you would like your congregation to pray for.
- Develop a planting or planter prayer calendar. Provide a monthly calendar that lists daily prayer concerns from church planters. A judicatory office can usually provide this.
- Pray 9-1-1. Have each person in the congregation list the name of one person who needs to be in relationship with Christ. Ask everyone to pray each day at 9:00 a.m. and 1:00 p.m. for that one person.
- Recruit a prayer team for the purpose of praying for church planting. There are people in your church who are gifted in prayer. Recruit them to a planting prayer team. Keep them informed as to needs. Give them names of planters. Provide a list of communities where a new church might be started or is starting.

- Take a prayer walk through your community, looking for locations where a new church might be started. Enlist a group who might come together on Saturday and walk parts of your community. As they do, have them pray.
- Ask your congregation for names of unsaved people, and begin a prayer list for them. These names could be placed on a wall or attached to a cross as a visual reminder that people need Christ.
- Ask people to come to the altar representing unsaved family, friends, and co-workers. Lay hands on them, praying for those they represent. Open the altar for this. It is a tangible way to keep those disconnected from Christ before your people. Making time in a service to do this highlights the importance of reaching people.
- Make a prayer meeting guideline that for every prayer asking for a physical touch, a prayer for a specific person who needs Christ must be included. This helps keep an inward and outward balance.
- Invite a church planter to your Sunday morning service and make a special time to lay hands on him or her. Hearing real people share real stories increases people's awareness and concern for church planters and their efforts.

The June 2006 issue of *Fast Company* told the story of EVP Miller who carries the title of Chief Disruption Officer for Herman Miller Office Furniture.[4] His role is to push the envelope of innovation. He is to keep the company on the edge of discontent by pushing them to forge ahead to new frontiers. It is easy for people or organizations to settle where they are. Keeping on the edge of discontent results in taking risks, making improvements, and asking how to do things better. This is what missional praying does. It acts as the chief disruption force keeping the church on the edge of discontent. Churches are to be missional forces multiplying believers, leaders, and churches. Prayer keeps driving us toward that end.

ACTION STEP

Here is a way to help generate prayer in your congregation. The goal will be to take time to get into the community for prayer and observation. The idea is to have God be the director and open the eyes of your people to potential opportunities.

Identify three or four communities, neighborhoods, villages, or towns within a five- to ten-mile radius of your church. Select a three-hour block on a Saturday (suggested time: 10:00 a.m.–1:00 p.m.). Have some people willing to prepare a lunch. Invite the congregation to meet at the church.

KEY POINTS

- Include planting in pastoral prayer.
- Include church planters in bulletin prayer section.
- Develop a planting or planter prayer calendar.
- Pray 9-1-1.
- Recruit a planting prayer team.
- Take a prayer walk through your community.
- Develop a prayer list for unsaved individuals.
- Have an open altar for those needing Christ.
- Balance prayer meetings with inward/outward needs.
- Invite a church planter to be prayed over.

Explain that groups will be sent out to various areas to explore potential planting locations. Divide those who showed up into groups of five to ten and assign each group an area to investigate.

Ask each group to walk its assigned area and pray for those living there. In addition, ask each group to think about and observe the following:

1. How does this area differ from the one where our church is located?
2. What is the lifestyle of the folks who live here?
3. How many churches are there nearby?
4. What spiritual sense did you get as you prayed?
5. What kind of church might be planted here?

6. How would the people you noticed fit in our church?
7. Do you sense you might be open to helping begin a church in this area?

Request that the groups be back at the church by noon. When they return, serve them lunch and have them discuss their findings. Finally, ask them to commit to pray for seven days for the community they scouted.

This is one method that might be used to implement prayer into this process. Getting the congregation focused on potential communities for church planting will galvanize future endeavors in the parenting process.

3 GIVE PROMOTION

I once read about a company that pays college students one hundred and fifty dollars per week to wear a temporary ad tattoo on their foreheads. My initial response was, "How did they think of that?" The times I have caught myself observing someone's forehead, I have to honestly say it never entered my mind to slap an ad up there.

Then the realization came. They saw foreheads as ad space because that is what they do—they advertise! And because they advertise, they see everything as potential to promote a product.

In parenting new churches, we need to do the same—promote! Promotion is a third way a church can participate in parenting a new church.

Promotion is drawing attention to church planting and church planters. It is a combination of public affirmation and prayer. It is a church's willingness to heighten the corporate awareness of starting new churches. A church that chooses to promote church planting will be on the constant look out for "foreheads" they can use for promotion.

Keeping church planting in the forefront of a congregation's thoughts takes effort. But it is this effort that will result in building excitement and enthusiasm. Promotion is more a matter of innovation than dollars. An environment can be created that will help a congregation to promote church planting. Promotion is not bells and whistles, but a sincere commitment to the task of helping start new churches.

> "Reproducing churches is the quickest way to win many people to our Lord Jesus Christ."
>
> George Patterson and Richard Scoggins

I saw the results of a survey in which people ninety-five years of age or older were asked this question: "What would you do differently if you could live your life over?" Three responses were shared most often:

1. They would spend more time getting away from the daily grind to thoughtfully examine the direction and meaning of their lives.

2. They would be more courageous about stepping out of their comfort zones.
3. They would do more things that would outlive them.

These responses can be applied to churches. Churches tend to shy away from thoughtful reflection. They hold on to their comfort zones. They tend to think more present than future. Yet helping start churches can address each of these issues. A church that helps start churches will be forced to reflect more deeply on the direction of their church. A church that helps start churches will have to move into uncomfortable zones. A church that helps start churches will be investing in what will outlive them, since the typical lifespan of a church is forty to sixty years. Recognizing the value of this will motivate a church to promote church planting as part of its strategic involvement.

> - How often does your leadership spend time reflecting on ministry effectiveness?
> - What are your church's comfort zones?
> - What is your church investing its energy in that will outlive it?

PROMOTION IS A FUNCTION OF LEADERSHIP

Churches make time for that which is important. And what is important to the church is typically what is important to the leader. Leadership is more than finding the motivation to propel people forward. It is courageous willingness to go first—to lead people into new realms. Promoting church planting contributes to this end. It puts in the fore of the congregation the challenging, but rewarding, opportunity that is church planting.

Parent church leaders have to shape mindsets. They have to get people to buy in to the reality that it is better to give than receive. They must help others move into the realm of sending out workers for the kingdom, not just gaining more members for their church. They must enable others to expand the horizons of their vision to encompass reaching people who may never enter the parent church and communities that may otherwise not be reached.

> "Leadership takes people from where they are to where they have never been."
>
> — Tom Clegg

If only things that happen in the church and for the church are promoted, this inward focus is the mindset that will be developed. However, if promotion is done regarding activities elsewhere and about things that may not directly help a particular local congregation, this will be a huge missional statement. But the church leaders must guide this. It will not just happen.

A newspaper ran a story of a single-engine plane that took off without a pilot. It flew for ninety minutes before running out of fuel and crashing. Apparently, the pilot had started the plane by hand-turning the propeller. The unsecured aircraft, upon starting, rolled down the runway leaving a dazed pilot behind. It took off and climbed to twelve thousand feet. It ended its journey by crashing into an open field. The observation was made that "It seems that the very worthy and capable vessel still needed a pilot."

Most churches are worthy and capable, but, if they are ever to help start a church, they need a leader (pilot) who will promote church planting. This person will keep them on the ragged edge of faith—that scary place where God is most needed—and will create new visions for the future. The new vision is for churches to grow and multiply. Such a vision is in need of leaders.

DISCUSSION
1. What does what you promote say about your church?
2. Based on the things the leadership gets enthusiastic about, what might the congregation say is your priority?
3. What can be done to promote kingdom events over local church events?

PROMOTION IS MORE AN ART THAN A SCIENCE

I recently came across this statement: "Life isn't a science; we make it up as we go along." Much the same can be said for promoting church planting. It is more an art than a science. How it is done is not nearly as important as that it be done. However, there are principles that can be useful in driving promotion of church planting.

The Porch Light Principle. I remember hot summer evenings as a kid watching moths attracted to our porch light. In the same way, promoting church planting attracts people's interest. Many in the congregation may never think of church planting at any level until it is brought up by church leadership.

> How you promote is not nearly as important as *that* you promote.

The Both/And Principle. Promotion is verbal and visual. It is written and illustrated. It is delivered in a variety of ways in a variety of circumstances. Don't be limited by either/or; strive for the benefit that both/and provides.

The Get Over Ourselves Principle. We think that if programming doesn't happen on our property it doesn't count for the kingdom. Therefore, we limit ourselves to promoting ministry tied to our facility. We have to recognize that not everything has to happen on our property. Once we get over ourselves, we will more readily promote new works.

The Rolex Principle. Timing is everything. Rolex makes one of the best watches. The Spirit of God provides the best timing. When promoting church planting, especially if it is new to your people, you'll need to plan as to when to promote it.

The Gumby Principle. Gumby was a little green clay character from an animated television show in the 1950s. He was flexible and moldable. In promotion, this is a necessity. You have to be flexible. Be innovative. Find fun and interesting ways to keep church planting before your people.

> **KEY POINTS**
> - Porch Light Principle
> - Both/And Principle
> - Get Over Ourselves Principle
> - Rolex Principle
> - Gumby Principle
> - Rabbit Principle

The Rabbit Principle. Rabbits are known for being prolific. Be prolific in your promotion of church planting. You can't promote it once and be done. You need to share church planting with your congregation over and over.

God will honor your commitment to keep church planting and church planters before your people. Don't get caught up in trying to promote just right; instead look for innovative methods and avenues to publicize church planting.

ASKING WHY NOT?

The organization had done the same thing each year. With little fanfare and limited promotion, the NFL began its season. The seasonal kick-off would begin Labor Day weekend. Not necessarily a great weekend to begin, but they were the NFL. This is the way they had always begun their season.

Just over six years ago, the conversation shifted. It moved from how we do things to what, why, and why not? Roger Goodell (current NFL commissioner) and John Wildhack (ESPN vice president) were having dinner together in a New York City restaurant. Goodell wanted to know what the NFL could do to "grab fans and drive TV viewers to games."[1] They knew there was a problem with simply starting the season. They wanted a big bang.

> What can you do to grab your congregation's attention?

Popular play-by-play announcer John Madden had complained that the NFL had little fanfare for opening day compared to Major League Baseball. In essence he was asking "why?" That got the conversation started and led to the exploration of new ideas. "Our cockamamie idea was why not do a Thursday night opener instead?" recalls Wildhack.

Looking back from the platform of success, the risk may not be appreciated. Thursday night was, and is, the biggest TV night of the week. It is the "home of blockbuster shows such as *Survivor* and *CSI* and the must-see TV night for the young viewers craved by networks."[2] Broadcasting football during this prized time slot was a bold move. The NFL's willingness to make this choice has paid off. Dick Ebersol observes, "They've [NFL] begun to own the landscape in September."

There is a road map in this story that can be helpful to the church; a road map that can guide us to discover and implement cockamamie promotional ideas. Truth be told, churches are mired in the *what* we do scenario. It is difficult to peer over the "always done" to a God-given vision; but it can be done.

Recognize the Problem. People and organizations will never change if they don't believe there is a reason for it. The NFL first had to recognize that what they were doing was not maximized; they wanted more exposure for the start of their season. Could they begin their season better? What are some of the challenges you have in communicating to the congregation? What predictable methods do you fall back on to get word out about upcoming events (for example pulpit announcements)? Look for areas that may be working, but not as well as they could. Search out new ways of saying routine things.

Have Something to Point to. The NFL pointed to baseball. By observing what baseball was doing, the NFL came up with an idea of what they might do. They were not baseball, so what they did would have to fit their sport. But they did not have to begin at square one. This applies to promoting ideas in church as well. Look around. Notice what other churches are doing. Talk to fellow pastors. How have they been able to communicate to their people? Take these ideas and apply them to church planting.

Consider Options. There are all kinds of ways to approach challenges. Throw them out there for consideration. We tend to be too careful. We want to pre-filter options. Resist this. What at first glance appears an un-doable idea may be the best idea.

KEY POINTS
- Recognize the problem.
- Have something to point to.
- Consider options.
- Try stuff.

Try Stuff. You never know what will work until you try. The NFL could have discussed the pros and cons of using a Thursday night game to start the season for a long time, but it wasn't until they tried it that they knew. Give those promotional ideas a try. You never know what will do the trick.

A FEW SUGGESTIONS

Here are a few suggestions of how to promote church planting. Don't take this as an exhaustive list. Instead use the ideas as fodder for the creation of more and better innovative ideas.

How can you effectively highlight church planting within your congregation?

- Display an area map in the foyer of the church with pins indicating the location of new churches.
- Host a church planting fair. Invite planters and planting organizations to share about their ministries.
- Invite a church planter to your church to preach on the biblical mandate to multiply.
- Have a Church Planting Sunday where all things church planting are highlighted.
- Invite members of a church planting core team to share why they felt called to help start a church.
- Show a DVD or video on church planting.
- Preach a sermon on the biblical values of church multiplication.
- Create a Wall of Fame in the church where pictures of church planters are displayed.

- Encourage people from your church to attend a new church. Interview them as to their impressions.
- Place church planting as a discussion point for at least half of your yearly leadership team meeting.
- Read a book on church planting. Share your thoughts with your leadership team.
- Hand out a packet of seeds to everyone on Sunday morning. Ask them to use it as a prayer reminder of new churches.
- Build a promotional team charged with keeping church planting before the congregation.
- Plant a tree on church property with a plaque identifying it as the planting tree.
- Show a video of a new church baptizing new converts.
- Interview charter members of your congregation. Let people know these were the core team of your church.

THE PARABLE OF THE MAGNOLIA TREE

My wife and I love trees. When we lived in Sacramento, we lived in a new neighborhood where mature trees were rare. We knew any tree we planted would provide more shade and climbing enjoyment for future generations than for us, but we planted trees anyway.

One of the trees we planted was a magnolia. We tried to plant it correctly. The hole was dug. The sapling was placed in the ground. We staked it for support as per instructions. We even ringed it with rocks, providing a more aesthetic environment. The nurturing process began as we imagined the mighty tree that it one day would become.

A few months after the magnolia was planted, our hopes diminished. The tree began looking none too healthy. We brought in an expert (a friend with a landscaping business) for a consultation. The verdict was too much water. Listening to the outside opinion, we cut back on the water. It was an action taken too late. The magnolia did not make it. An empty rock ring resided where a potential healthy tree once stood.

Interestingly enough, at the same time, only a few feet away another new tree was making great progress. Our attention was so focused on the magnolia that we hadn't immediately noticed this new addition to our yard. It was a tree we hadn't planted. Instead, it was the result of another tree.

On the other side of our fence stood a nondescript tree, planted by the developer as a part of community landscaping. Evidently a seed, a sprig, or whatever was necessary, blew off the parent tree and into our yard. It found itself a place to grow and flourish. The parent tree did naturally what we were unsuccessful at doing artificially. This tree would be providing shade and climbing for future generations.

I spent many mornings looking at that growing tree. I marveled at its resilience. I wondered at the natural process of one tree planting another. I thought of it in terms of a missional multiplication movement.

> The best time to plant a tree was twenty years ago; the next best time is now.

Our yard was like a judicatory. We had defined an area for which we were responsible. It was our desire to make it an enjoyable place. It needed to be a place where plants and trees could grow. We wanted it to provide peace and comfort for others. We could make of it what we wished. It was for us to provide an environment where life flourished.

Our planting of the magnolia tree was like a judicatory church plant. We took all the right steps. We put it in a location where we believed it would add value. We attempted to do all that was necessary to make it live and thrive. We invested our dreams and wishes, but in our situation the plant did not survive. When judicatories plant churches, sometimes the new churches make it; sometimes they don't. Judicatories may not plant churches as well as local churches do, but it doesn't mean they should not give it a try.

The tree on the other side of the fence was like a local church that naturally and easily invested itself into another place. The investment paid dividends. A new church was started—one that provided in a new place what the parent never could. The judicatory (yard) provided the soil and environment necessary to help the church grow, but the parent tree invested the key ingredients.

The parable of the magnolia tree teaches us several things:

1. Judicatories can plant churches, but not as effectively as other churches can.
2. Existing churches will plant churches naturally if they are healthy and free to release resources.
3. Judicatories can, and should, provide the soil and environment for churches to plant churches.

4. New churches may not make it, but that doesn't mean we should stop planting.
5. Churches should be free to plant churches across fences (denominational and judicatory lines).
6. Regardless of how they are started, new churches make life more enjoyable.
7. New churches must be seen as an investment in the future, not only valuable for the present.

The local church is the hope of new churches. Without the local church, new churches are more vulnerable. With the support of a local church, new churches are more viable.

DISCUSSION QUESTIONS

1. Which of the lessons from the magnolia tree can you learn from?

2. In what yard might you make an investment?

GIVE PROMOTION

3. What is your opinion of churches starting new churches compared to judicatories starting new churches?

RESOURCES
- *The Speed of Trust* by Stephen M.R. Covey, Stephen R. Covey, and Rebecca R. Merrill.
- *The Churching of America* by Roger Finke and Rodney Stark.
- *God's Missionary People* by Charles E. Van Engen.

GENEROUSLY PROVIDE 4

Every step we take generates six to eight watts of energy, which then dissipates into thin air. According to *Fast Company* magazine, an innovative architectural firm in London is looking to capture this energy on a mass scale and turn it into electricity.

Claire Price of Facility Architects says, "At Victoria Station, you have 34,000 people traveling through in one hour. If you harness that energy . . . you can actually generate a very useful power source." This firm is looking at developing vibration-harvesting sensors. "These devices would be embedded into the structure of train stations, bridges, factories, or any other building frequently rattled by commuters, vehicles, or machinery. The devices would capture . . . [and] convert [the vibrations] into useable electricity."[1]

This unique way of finding resources exemplifies the fourth way churches might participate in starting a new church. The provision for starting new churches resides in existing churches. Just like the energy to fuel our world resides in people and structures, so the fuel needed for a missional multiplication movement is embedded in existing churches.

CHARACTERISTICS OF A CHURCH THAT PROVIDES

> What is given, and how it is given, dictates the return.

At our previous home, we had a succession of trees in our front yard. These were all of the beginning type—think sapling. We would bring them home in a plastic bucket. Following the planting instructions, we would replant them in the yard. They always began strong, but over time they slowly dried up.

We were on our third tree. I was aggressively and expertly—I thought—trimming the grass from around the base of the tree. My neighbor, watching my technique, said, "You know you are killing your tree." He could tell by the shocked look on my face that I had no idea how he could make such a determination. He continued, "The weed whacker is removing the bark. The tree loses its ability to gain nourishment if the bark is damaged."

"You mean," I inquired tentatively, "I am a tree killer?"

"Pretty much," was his unemotional response.

It had been me the entire time. My actions resulted in our inability to nurture a tree. A tree's ability to survive is dependent on having a place to grow, sufficient water, good soil, and protection from well-intentioned lawn caretakers. A properly cared-for tree grows.

Much like a tree needs a variety of conditions to flourish, new churches need a favorable environment in which to develop. Existing churches have the ability to provide such a climate by becoming a providing church.

Not all churches are able to supply the necessary environment. In order for a church to be a successful providing church for new church plants, the parent church must possess some key characteristics.

Healthy Constitution. Providing churches are healthy churches. Health assessment instruments, such as the

Church Health Profile, or the Natural Church Development Survey from New Church Specialties, can be helpful in determining a church's strengths and weaknesses.

Corporately Self-Assured. Providing churches have confidence. They have a strong sense of call. They know what they are about, and they want to be about investing in opportunities outside themselves.

Internal Multiplying Systems. Churches that help start churches have their own internal systems for multiplying ministries. Leaders, small groups, Sunday school classes, and worship services are all built to multiply. These churches understand that multiplication is the only guaranteed method of positive development.

360-Degree Vision. A providing church has developed a full vision. It sees all around itself. It is looking for ways to impact areas all around it. Seeing with 360-degree vision magnifies the necessity for new and different churches.

Opportunistic Climate. A providing church will try a variety of ways to help start churches. Providing churches realize learning is best accomplished by doing. Churches may fail when they do so; but they will develop experience. Failure is a method of growth, because failure is leveraged into learning.

Missional Passion. Providing churches see themselves as missionary outposts. Missional passion manifests itself in mobilization strategies. It is always about investing resources, never about keeping them.

Saint Matthew Lutheran Church is located in Walnut Creek, California. It is a church with missional passion. On its home page you are confronted with this message: "We say it with regularity and without wavering: Saint Matthew is a church on a mission. As a missionary congregation, bringing people to Christ and growing them in their faith, we must understand ourselves as partners in that mission and not just members."[2] Such an attitude fosters a climate where investing can be developed.

Stewardship of Generosity. Providing churches are generous churches. They take to heart the admonition of 2 Corinthians 9:11—"You will be made rich in every way so that you can be generous on every occasion." They are not just good stewards; they are generous stewards. They invest outside themselves with thankfulness. We will look at how to develop generosity a bit later.

Avoid the Survivor Mentality. The reality TV craze is in full force. The pioneer of this genre is *Survivor*. A group of people is placed in an exotic location. The goal is simple. Don't get voted off! The winner is the one who survives all the votes.

A providing church is not concerned with survival at the expense of the mission. Too many churches have circled the wagons and made survival the issue. This results in limited energy, vision, and achievement. A providing church has the attitude of Esther: "If I perish, I perish" (Esther 4:16). Providing churches measure effectiveness by what has been multiplied, not what has been maintained.

New church saplings are ready to be planted. What is needed is the climate to nurture and enhance their growth.

KEY POINTS

- Healthy Constitution
- Corporately Self-Assured
- Internal Multiplying Systems
- 360-Degree Vision
- Opportunistic Climate
- Missional Passion
- Stewardship of Generosity
- Avoid the Survivor Mentality

THE G-FORCE

Provision is a corporate response to the resources needed by church plants and church planters. Provision is an act of generosity. A church that has not cultivated a generous spirit will not participate in providing for starting churches. Generosity is a choice.

The movie *Space Cowboys* is about four former astronauts, now senior adults, training to go into space. Two of the characters, played by Tommy Lee Jones and Clint Eastwood, had invested a lifetime competing against each other. In one scene, they were in the NASA simulator that produced gravitational pull. Their competition was to see who would pass out first due to the increased pressure caused by the g-force (gravitational force). Frankly, I don't remember who won. It might have been a tie. The point I want to make is, they were overcome by the g-force.

- How would you describe the generosity of your church?
- How has the congregation shown itself generous?

The g-force is a critical component of provision. In this application it refers to the generosity force. The g-force applies positive pressure to churches, compelling them to share resources for starting new, growing, healthy, multiplying churches. Inherent in the parenting process is a willingness to hold resources lightly and to invest beyond the needs of one local church.

There are three essential understandings that a church must adopt if it is to be drawn in by the g-force.

Generosity is an Attitude. Generosity is not an amount. Churches can kid themselves into thinking that if they had more they could do more. Jesus rearranged such thinking when he applauded the woman who gave what she had. She had an attitude of generosity, regardless of the amount.

I am often asked, "How much do we need to invest to help start a church?" My response is, "Do what you can. Just be clear about communicating your commitments on the front end to the team that is beginning the church." A parent church can only do what it can do. If it is being drawn in by the g-force, it will take an honest inventory of resources and share liberally from what it has.

Generosity Can Be Cultivated. Like people, not all churches are naturally generous. However, leaders can cultivate this attitude. This can be cultivated by leaders who model a generous spirit. Teaching regularly on this topic underscores its importance.

Generosity Begins With What You Have. I have known many generous people, and they all had this in common—they did not wait until some future time to bless others with what they had; they did it now. If you have the attitude that you will be generous someday, you likely never will.

You don't have to wait for anything. Know that God desires for you to be a generous congregation. There may be a sense that you want to start a church. Wonderful! Start now. Begin where you are with what you have.

> **KEY POINTS**
> - Generosity is an attitude.
> - Generosity can be cultivated.
> - Generosity begins with what you have.

PREPARING FOR PROVISION

Provision comes in three primary areas: people, finances, and real equity. People are a huge resource in church planting. A church that is willing to release people to serve elsewhere provides all kinds of potential for a new church. This will be addressed in more detail in chapter five. Bobby Knight, the former Texas Tech head basketball coach,

> **DISCUSSION**
> What can be done to prepare for helping to start new churches?

has been credited with saying, "The will to prepare is more important than the will to win." Abraham Lincoln mentioned to a colleague, after one of his many political defeats, "I will prepare, and my time will come." The bottom line is that preparation should not be underestimated.

The same can be said for churches. A congregation may want to jump right into helping start churches. This desire may cause them to leap headlong into the fray. They may move so quickly that they do help, but the result is negative for them and the church they help establish. Instead, they should involve themselves in preparation. A rightly prepared church will be a better provider.

What are some preparations a church might use?

Leaders Are Developed. A church positioning itself to help start churches will not be content with existing leaders. There will be a conscious effort to identify, train, and release leaders. Pastoral staff, board members, Sunday school teachers, small group leaders, ushers, and every ministry position will be mentoring and monitoring potential leaders. This rich leadership environment allows for easier transitions when churches are started. The parent church has people to step in when others are called to step out.

Evangelism is Reflected. It's reflected in the fabric of ministry. The church is actively involved in reaching its community. Programs are designed to fulfill the Great Commission. People are equipped to share their faith with friends and family. The leaders model evangelism. When evangelism is woven throughout the life of the church, multiplication will happen.

Ministry is Driven by Mission. The mission informs the ministry, instead of the ministry informing the mission. The mission is the guiding force. No ministry is begun unless it helps accomplish the mission. Ministries that no longer have mission value are discontinued. This is not viewed as failure, but as a refinement process that will stop drift. Three questions are regularly asked and answered:

- Do our people know the mission?
- Do our people know their role in fulfilling the mission?
- What feedback are we giving our people concerning the fulfillment of the mission?

Prayer Is a Core Value. Prayer is not just talked about; it is practiced. There are prayer teams, prayer partners, prayer training, and prayer feedback. Prayer is not a service add-on; it is central. Prayer reflects a congregation's understanding that they are desperately dependent on God. A praying church gets burdened for the magnitude of the task.

Generosity is Observable. The church treats its pastor and staff well. Love offerings are taken with joy when the opportunity presents itself. Hospitality is valued. A generous church is open with what it has, even though it may have little. A generous church will naturally share its resources through planting. A generous church will regularly ask, "How do we help start new works?"

DISCUSSION
What congregational lifestyle habits are being developed?

Ron Swor is the lead pastor of New Life Foursquare Church in Canby, Oregon. Over fifteen years ago he came to this church. They were running one hundred in weekly attendance. He wanted to start churches. He wanted to begin lifestyle habits in the church that would position them for multiplication. One of the first things he did was take an offering to buy chairs for a church planting friend. This offering more than covered the cost of chairs. This became the beginning of developing a multiplying church.

KEY POINTS
- Leaders are developed.
- Evangelism is reflected.
- Ministry is driven by mission.
- Prayer is an actual core value.
- Generosity is observable.

Since then, Ron has led his church in starting ten churches and adopting thirty others. In November 2001, New Life dedicated a new worship facility. The second week in this new facility, they commissioned three church planters and their teams. These teams were compromised of three hundred people and represented ten thousand dollars in monthly giving. They were able to do this in 2001 because of what they began in 1988. Ron shared, "Planting churches reminds me I don't have a corner on God's market."

> "Planting churches reminds me I don't have a corner on God's market."
> — Ron Swor

PROVISION IDEAS

Providing resources may seem like a daunting prospect, but it is easily accomplished if thought of as a series of smaller tasks. This is the attitude of a church that chooses to give provision to new churches—one step at a time. What you are able to provide initially may be a far cry from what you will be providing later. The idea is to start. Provide something.

FINANCES

When I was in youth ministry we did fundraisers each year to help students get to camp. Some of the dollars raised were placed in a special fund for those who needed scholarships. We wanted to do all we could to ensure that money would not be a barrier to those who needed the assistance.

We had an application process for camp scholarships. One year I was approached by the mom of a young person in the youth group. She came to inquire about a potential scholarship for her child. Her words were (and you can't make this stuff up), "We just purchased a boat, so we don't have the funds to send our child to camp. Could we get a scholarship?"

Her request was laughable. I did not see the strain a boat purchase placed on the family as an adequate foundation for granting a camp scholarship. Her child did not get the scholarship, but somehow they made ends meet to get their child to camp anyway.

People typically do what is necessary to get what they deem important. The same is true for churches. They will find money to help with what they genuinely deem important. Don't believe you are unable to help invest dollars in the starting of a new church. You have more resources than you might think.

Teach Generosity. Teach your people to give beyond themselves. A generous church knows sacrifice and the joy of what is enough when sharing with others. One practical means of teaching this is to take a special offering for the purpose of giving it away.

Ten Percent Rule. Most churches have the ability to roll over some funds each month. In other words, they do not expend every dollar collected in a given month. Take 10 percent of this amount and put it into a church plant fund.

Ten Percent Rule Redux. It is not unusual for churches to end the fiscal year with money in the general fund. Take ten percent of this money and include it in a church planting fund.

Put it in the Budget. Add a church planting line item in your yearly budget. Treat it like a bill. Pay it monthly.

Set Up a Memorial. How often do we see memorial funds for buildings? Why not have memorial funds for planting? When people ask to give in honor of someone, let them give to church planting.

Special Day Offering. Choose certain Sundays throughout the year to collect a special offering for church planting.

Examples might be: Super Bowl Sunday, Easter, Christmas Eve service, or on any fifth Sunday of a month.

These are a few suggestions to get you started. A little, invested over time, will result in an abundance of resources. Add to the list. Get creative.

REAL EQUITY

Real equity is tangible gifts of supplies, equipment, and promotional material. It is the stuff needed to help a church get started. Here are some ideas:

Ask the church planter for a list of supplies needed. Print them on a bulletin insert and ask your people to select ones they will purchase.

Throw a baby shower for the new church. Have a cake, punch, and games. Invite people to bring gifts for the new church.

Underwrite the first big promotional event they do. Lots of churches use big events to launch. Offer to underwrite this.

Provide all their copy needs for three months, six months, or one year. Allow them to use your paper and your copier.

Purchase big dollar items such as sound equipment, a projector, chairs, staging, etc. Or give the new church a gift card to a major electronics chain.

Fill the nursery. If they plan to have a ministry to young families, they will need a quality nursery. Make sure they have the best.

Underwrite the insurance for one year. This could be the health insurance for the planter, liability for the property they use, or whatever other insurance needs they may have.

> Real equity is tangible gifts of supplies, equipment, and promotional material.

Start a registry at a supply store. This could be for office, teaching, discipleship, or whatever ongoing needs they might have for resources.

One last word: do not give a new church your hand-me-downs. They are starting a tremendous adventure. They need to begin with the best you can offer.

RESOURCES

- Church Health Profile (www.churchhealthprofile.com).
- Natural Church Development Survey (www.newchurchspecialties.org).
- *Attitudes That Attract Success* by Wayne Cordeiro.
- *Funding Your Ministry* by Scott Morton.
- *The Shape of Things to Come* by Michael Frost and Alan Hirsch.
- *Leading Strategic Change* by J. Stewart Black and Hal B. Gregersen.

GRANT PERMISSION

In the generation following World War II, a major denomination started a new church in a region of the country where they had never had congregations before. It was a reproducing church from the beginning. It would regularly send out groups from its congregation to start new churches throughout the region. It would also sponsor, nest, or adopt new congregations of its denomination that began to emerge from other efforts.

More than fifty years later, almost three hundred churches of this denomination now exist within a fifty-mile radius of where this congregation started. According to George W. Bullard, Jr. and his study of a major Protestant, "More than 80 percent of the congregations are primarily composed of non-Anglo Americans, making this one of the most culturally diverse regions of this denomination in North America.[1]

This story illustrates what can happen when a church and its leadership catch a vision for its region and invests itself in the starting of new churches. A church willing to give permission to its people to participate in starting new congregations will see fruit beyond its dreams. A leader who encourages people to be open to God's leading in starting new congregations, and who grants permission to follow that leading even if it means leaving the parent church, will multiply ministry effectiveness many times over.

> A church willing to give permission to its people to participate in the starting of new congregations will see fruit beyond its dreams.

Giving permission for a church to help start new churches is the most challenging of the five ways to participate in starting new churches, because it's potentially the most costly. It demands faith and trust. It is acting on the belief that God is sovereign. It is the belief that a church cannot out-give God.

GIVE OR GO

Permission is manifested in two areas: giving and going. People must have permission to respond to God. They must know it is expected and desirable to participate in God's birthing of new congregations.

A Call to Go. When I led Arcade Wesleyan Church in Sacramento, California, in parenting churches I would say to my people, "Some of you are going to be called to help start a new church, and you don't even know it yet!" With that statement, and many like it, I was letting them know they had permission to be available to help start a new work. Permission is the willingness of the leader to release people to go.

The call to go may be for a long or short time. The call of a missionary can be applied to church planting. A person's call to go might be as a career worker, short-termer, or work-team member. The call could find several expressions.

> **DISCUSSION**
> - When you think of people going to a new church, what emotions does this bring out?
> - What do you believe would happen if people in your congregation began giving to a new church?

A Vocational Call. The individuals are called to go from your church to invest the rest of their lives in that new work. They have no plan to return to the parent church. They feel compelled to choose between remaining at the parent church or going to the new church. This may be the most difficult of the calls.

A Seasonal Call. The individuals are called for a certain time. We asked our people to consider a seasonal call. Would they give one year to help start this new church? After that year, they were free to return to the parent church. What we discovered, however, is that most seasonal calls turned into vocational calls. When folks did return from a seasonal call we would interview them much like we might those returning from the mission field. Their reports from the field helped prepare the hearts of future workers God would be calling.

A Work-Team Call. The individuals are called to give a certain skill to the new church. The sound technician goes to train the new sound team. The Sunday school teacher goes and provides teaching skills. The commercial real estate person helps negotiate a lease. There are many areas where individuals can offer their talents.

Those called vocationally or seasonally are a part of the core team. The work-team people typically make themselves available for a specific time, for a specific task.

Some words of advice regarding those who are seasonally called don't hold their place in line. What do I mean? Often when a person from a congregation commits to a plant for a specific time frame, the sending church might be tempted to hold his or her place. In other words, whatever the ministry area, you save it for his or her return. This is a mistake on two levels: (1) you don't allow God to raise new people in your congregation for tasks; and (2) you spend time waiting for their return instead of moving toward your future.

In both scenarios the church chooses to idle instead of shift into a new gear and move ahead. When the person returns there will be a place for them. Probably a much better place as the church will have grown and progressed, and they will have done the same.

> **KEY POINTS**
> - Vocational Call
> - Seasonal Call
> - Work-Team Call

INVESTMENT GIVING

Permission also encompasses a leader's willingness to encourage people to give. Giving is investing one's finances to help with a new church. Where provision is a corporate response, permission to invest personal finances is a personal response. The people are asked to inquire of God: "What, if anything, do you want our family to financially invest?" This could be a one-time gift. It could be an investment of all or part of their tithe. The tithe investment is for whatever time frame the people feel led. It is trusting God to guide them and provide for the permission-giving church.

This permission giving is a great opportunity to test a leader's faith. The reality is that most leaders are unwilling to trust God for what they expect their people to trust God. For example, a pastor has no problem saying to the congregation: "Give God the first 10 percent (tithe), and God will use the 90 percent to meet 100 percent of your needs." This is said with confidence and the full authority of Scripture, and rightly so. However, challenge pastors to trust God to fund new churches with their people's tithe and also care for their congregation, and the response is different. It is typically, "We could never do that and continue our ministry."

> Most leaders are unwilling to trust God despite the fact that they expect their people to do so.

A principle is a principle or it is not. God will either honor his Word or he will not. When we give, God will provide, or he will not. You can't have it both ways. If you expect your people to trust God individually, you had better trust God corporately. If you are not willing, you may want to rethink how you really feel about God's promises.

THREE THINGS TO THINK ABOUT

First, only the lead pastor can give his or her people permission to give or go. If it is not your vision, it will not translate to your people. The permission must be heartfelt. The leader needs to expect people to respond. They will need to be encouraged when they do.

Second, everyone is called. When it comes to church planting everyone in the congregation is called. Some are called to stay and strengthen the permission-giving church. Others are called to go and grow the new church. Clarifying it in these terms communicates that everyone has a role.

Third, never decide for your people. Leaders may jump to the conclusion that if a church being started is some distance away, people will not respond to going. None of us knows this. When we give people permission to listen to God, we will be amazed at what he calls them to do.

KEY POINTS
- Only the lead pastor can give people permission to give or go.
- Everyone is called.
- Never decide for your people.

PERMISSION-GIVING CULTURE

A willingness to give people permission to give and go does not happen automatically. Nor is it automatic that people will respond in a permission-giving environment. As an environment can be created to nurture a healthy crop, a church can work on developing a culture that produces people willing to respond to God's call.

Three cultivators are useful in developing a permission-giving culture: the heart of the leader; the vision of the leader; the priority of the task.

THE HEART OF THE LEADER

The heart describes passion, commitment, and the will of the individual. The spark can as easily be fanned into a fire of enthusiasm as it can be doused with the water of discouragement. Heart is the central drive of a permission-giving leader. A driving force may be God's love for a world in desperate need of his un-earnable grace. This heartfelt force will fuel forward progress. It is needed for a church to multiply.

A parent church leader's heart is passionate about churches being mobilized to see beyond themselves. We need to be committed to multiply congregations regardless of the cost. We need to be full of unbridled enthusiasm to make an impact beyond the property lines of one church in one location.

This heart cannot be delegated. It is not an optional accessory for leading a congregation toward parenting. The parenting leader must possess it personally. He or she must settle the issue and then invite others to participate.

As has often been noted, people don't latch onto worthy causes as quickly as they follow worthy leaders who espouse those causes.

> "People don't at first follow worthy causes. They follow worthy leaders who promote worthwhile causes."
>
> John Maxwell

How do you cultivate such a heart? Here are five practical steps:

Cultivate the Soil of Your Soul. I lived in Rocklin, California. The name was an apt description of the land in our community. I can testify that every time a shovel or pick was put into the ground, a rock would be hit. It would appear that such ground could never support trees or shrubs. However, when properly cultivated, it provided fertile soil for all kinds of growth. The same is true of our souls. They may be rocky and appear counterproductive to parenting.

Yet, the proper cultivation can soften the soul to the openness of a parenting vision.

The Spirit of God is the best tilling tool available. Spend time with God. Listen to his voice. Put yourself in regular positions of having your life intersect with him.

Connect With Others. Get around people who will infect you with the vision to parent. I can remember when my oldest child brought chicken pox home from school. He even shared it with his two younger siblings. When word got out that we had pox at home, you would assume people would want to stay away. Quite the contrary! We got phone calls from parents wanting to bring their preschool kids to the house. Why? They wanted them infected. They wanted them to get chicken pox to inoculate them before they went to school. The principle: close proximity increases the likelihood of shared participation.

The principle works! Get around leaders who have the infection you want. Increase your exposure to church parenting carriers. It will rub off. You will begin to catch the germ. And don't treat yourself with the back-to-typical-church antibiotics.

Chart Your Course. God will birth a permission-giving plan in your heart. Write down your God-given dream. Put it in a concise paragraph. Develop a one-sentence vision statement that captures your dream. Keep the big picture in mind.

Construct Your Next Steps. Charting involves drawing the big strokes. Construction involves giving attention to details. It is building the plan. It is putting resources together. Then the next steps provide progress. Oswald Sanders communicated this succinctly: "Vision without a plan is dreaming; a plan without a vision is drudgery; a vision plus a plan equals direction."

Celebrate the Fulfillment of the Dream. It may not be obvious today, but there will be a celebration. Rejoice in the methods by which God reveals himself in this process. Rejoice that your church is being used to build the kingdom.

KEY POINTS

- Cultivate the soil of your soul.
- Connect with others.
- Chart your course.
- Construct your next steps.
- Celebrate the fulfillment of the dream.

THE VISION OF THE LEADER

A leader who has vision has the ability to see things before they happen. That vision is a critical first step in bringing any new thing into existence. This is the essence of vision—seeing later, now. This is what is needed in the hearts of leaders who desire to expand the kingdom of God. Vision calls leaders beyond the confines of one local church to seeing multiple churches started—new churches that in time will spawn other churches.

Vision can be cultivated. It must expand a leader's heart to envision entire regions captured for God. It must expand a leader's heart to see diverse churches raised up to meet diverse needs. It must expand a leader's heart to see people mobilized to start multiplying churches.

CULTIVATE A VISION

Dare to Dream. Make the choice to go beyond yourself. Determine to see more than the ministries growing and expanding in your existing location. Envision all kinds of churches being started to reach all kinds of people using all kinds of methods.

Develop the Dream. Get yourself ready. Put things in place to see the dream of multiplying churches become a reality.

You may not be ready to parent a church today, but you must prepare for tomorrow. List potential areas to begin new churches. Get around like-minded leaders. Begin an initial plan to multiply churches out of your congregation.

Deliver the Dream. This is making it happen.

Disperse the Dream. This is making others part of the dream by sharing ownership with them. It is expanding involvement to a wide range of leaders. When others participate, the dream becomes greater than any one person could hope.

PRIORITY OF THE TASK

Jerry was consistently inconsistent in his church attendance. He loved the people. He loved the church. I believe he even liked me as his pastor. Yet, none of this got him to attend regularly.

One day he came by the church office. I had the opportunity to chat with him. I let him know he had been missed. He told me the ramping up of his new carpet-cleaning business was keeping him busy. He was working long hours. He was tired and often, it was a challenge to get to church.

My assistant pastor happened by and entered our conversation. Our discussion moved to golf. Jerry was an avid golfer. My assistant and I spoke about the possibility of golfing in the future. In the midst of that conversation a transformation happened in Jerry's schedule. It got room! His energy increased, and he said, "When are you golfing? I can golf!"

What happened? Jerry revealed his priorities. As busy and tired as he was, there could be time for golf.

If a church is going to be a multiplying church, multiplication must be a priority. Why should local churches make multiplication a priority? One word: mission. Churches need to be about mission. Churches need to recognize the tremendous need in our world today. A need so great that if established churches do not spearhead the planting of multiplying congregations we will fall short of the effectiveness God intends for us.

I have heard it said, "The longest journey begins with the first step." You need to take the STEPS necessary to move toward church parenting as a ministry priority.

PRIORITY STEPS

Seek Prayer. This priority must be birthed and developed in prayer. The pastor must settle it first. The lay leadership needs to be led in praying toward this end.

Target an Area. Begin now to consider where a new missional church might be started.

Evaluate the Present Health of Your Church. Growing, healthy churches will multiply. Therefore, prioritizing permission-giving will necessitate occasional church health checkups. Many churches have benefited from using church health inventories. Find one that works and use it.

Prepare Today For Tomorrow. You may not be ready to parent today, but what are you doing now to prepare for the day when you will plant? Two things that can be done to prepare for that tomorrow are (1) putting resources (books, workshop information, etc.) on church

DISCUSSION
- What significant section of the local population is missing from your church (e.g., families, men, seniors, youth)?
- How might you start a specialized work aimed toward this missing sector?
- What area in your community does your current style of ministry not reach effectively?
- What surrounding communities have people who drive thirty minutes or more, one way, to attend your church?

multiplication in the hands of your leaders, and (2) preaching a sermon series on church multiplication.

Spirit Directed. The Spirit of God must direct this endeavor. "Since we live by the Spirit, let us keep in step with the Spirit" (Gal. 5:25). Spirit responsiveness is mission critical. God will direct your steps.

THE CURE FOR HICCUPS

A woman went to a clinic. She was seen by one of the new doctors in the group. After a few minutes in the examination room, she burst out screaming and ran down the hall.

An older doctor, who had treated her many times over the years, stopped her and asked what the problem was. She explained. Her explanation caused a disturbed, almost angry look to cross his face. He attempted to calm her down as he led her into another room to rest. He informed her that he would be right back.

The older doctor shoved open the door and marched down the hall. He aggressively entered the room where he found the young doctor writing on a chart. "What's the matter with you? Mrs. Jones is seventy-two years old!

She has six grown children and fifteen grandchildren. What were you thinking telling her she was pregnant?"

The young doctor smiled smugly as he continued to make notes on the chart. Without looking up he said, "Cured her hiccups, didn't it?"

His methods may have been unorthodox, but he did get results. Permission-giving churches can be like this. Unorthodox methods are used to accomplish desired results. When it comes to church multiplication, we need to explode preconceived ideas of how churches must be started. A church parenting and planting movement is dependent on existing churches giving permission for people to give and to go.

> What keeps you from giving permission to your people to give and go?

God wants to birth innovative, creative, line breaking, and unreasonable methods of starting new churches. Will you give your people permission to participate? Or will you pull back? The choice is yours.

RESOURCES

- *Big Dreams in Small Places* by Tom Nebel.
- *Churches Starting Churches* by Bill Sullivan.
- *Lost in America* by Tom Clegg and Warren Bird.

NOTES

Introduction
1. Ed Stetzer, *Planting Missional Churches* (Nashville: Broadman and Holman Publishers, 2006), 38.

1. Go Public
1. Lecture by Dave Olson at Mission America Coalition Conference, Kansas City, Mo., October 2007.
2. Ibid.
3. Ed Stetzer, *Planting New Churches in a Postmodern Age* (Nashville: Broadman and Holman Publishers, 2003), 6.

2. Generate Prayer
1. Bobby Ghosh, "Life in Hell: A Baghdad Diary," *Time*, August 6, 2006.
2. Dawson Trotman quoted in Josh Hunt's *Let It Grow*, (Grand Rapids: Baker Book House, 1993), 64.
3. Becky Tirabassi, *Let Prayer Change Your Life Workbook* (Nashville: Thomas Nelson, 1995).
4. Linda Tischler, "Herman Miller's Leap of Faith," Fast Company online edition (June 2006), http://www.fastcompany.com/magazine/106/herman-miller.html.

3. Go Public
1. Michael McCarthy, "Early blitz, glitz make extra points for NFL," *USAToday* online, (September 6, 2006), http://www.usatoday.com/sports/football/nfl/2006-09-06-kickoff-business_x.htm.
2. Ibid.

4. Generously Provide
1. Tracy Staedter, "Good Viobrations," *Fast Company* online edition, (September 2006), http://www.fastcompany.com/magazine/108/next-artifact-future.html.
2. "About Us," Saint Matthew Lutheran Church, http://www.saintmatthew.org/aboutus/a_home.htm (accessed March 28, 2008).

5. Grant Permission
1. George W. Bullard Jr., "Pursuing the Full Kingdom Potential of Your Congregation," (St. Louis: Chalice Press, 2006), 11–12.